Exploring the World of Astronomy

by George Burns
illustrated by Nancy Woodman

A *Try This* Book
Franklin Watts
New York * Chicago * London * Toronto * Sydney

Cover art by Nancy Woodman

Photographs copyright ©:
National Optical Astronomy Observatories: p. 8;
Photo Researchers, Inc.: pp. 9 (Douglas Faulkner), 23, 29 (both David Parker/SPL),
34 (Jerry Schad), 39 (McGrath/SPL); Comstock, Inc.: pp. 14, 19 (Stuart Cohen),
26 (Russ Kinne); Hale Observatories: p. 45

Library of Congress Cataloging-in-Publication Data

Burns, George, 1953–
Exploring the world of astronomy / by George Burns :
illustrated by Nancy Woodman.
p. cm. — (Try this!)
Includes index.
ISBN 0-531-20124-4 – ISBN 0-531-15745-8 (pbk.)
1. Astronomy—Juvenile literature. 2. Astronomy—Experiments
Juvenile literature. [1. Astronomy—Experiments.
2. Experiments.] I. Woodman, Nancy, ill. II. Title. III. Series: Try this series.
QB46.B945 1995
520—dc20
94-49442   CIP AC

Exploring
the World
of Astronomy

CONTENTS

THE WORLD OF ASTRONOMY

Have you ever looked up at the night sky and wondered about the twinkling stars? What are they doing up there? What do they look like up close?

Or maybe you've simply wondered why the moon can be seen on some nights, but not others. Why does it seem to constantly change shape? If you have ever asked yourself questions like these, then you have already taken your first steps to becoming an *astronomer*. (To learn how to pronounce a word in italics, look in the glossary in the back of the book.)

Astronomy is the study of the stars, the planets, and all the other things in space. Many astronomers work with enormous *telescopes*, computers, and instruments that gather radio waves from space.

It would be fascinating to use that kind of equipment, but you can just as easily be an astronomer without it. The activities in this book will help you be an astronomer. You will explore some very important ideas in astronomy with everyday materials.

An astronomer observes the sky through telescopes in observatories like this one.

✳ ✳ ✳ ✳ ✳ ✳ ✳ ✳ ✳ ✳ ✳ ✳ ✳ ✳

One thing professional astronomers do is keep careful records of their work. You may want to get a notebook or pad to keep track of all the activities you do from this book. Be an astronomer and try these activities!

THE SUN

When we think about stars, we usually think about blinking lights against a dark night sky. But our closest star—and the one we see most often—is visible only during the day. That star is the Sun.

The Sun gives us heat and light.

Like all stars, the Sun is a massive ball of exploding gases and fire. The energy from the Sun is so strong that it heats our planet from 93 million miles away. The Sun's light is so bright that looking at the Sun for just a few seconds can damage your eyes. **Never look directly at the Sun!**

How can we prove that the Sun's rays are giving us heat? What kind of experiences have you had that tell you we are getting heat from the Sun?

Try This: ✳ ✳ ✳ ✳ ✳ ✳ ✳ ✳ ✳ ✳

Make a list of all the ways you can think of to prove that the warmth we feel outside during the day comes from the Sun.

Do this activity on a sunny day. Cut four pieces of cardboard to a size of about 6 inches by 10 inches (15 centimeters by 25 centimeters) each. If you don't have cardboard, stiff paper will do. You could use manila folders, for example.

Cover one side of each piece of cardboard with aluminum foil. It may help to tape the foil to the edges of the cardboard. Try to keep the aluminum foil smooth. It will work better if you do.

Fill a small glass or clear plastic cup halfway up with cool water. Take the *temperature* of the water with an air temperature *thermome-*

ter. Write the time and the temperature in your notebook.

Leave the cup in a sunny spot. Wait about 15 minutes. Take the water temperature again and write it down with the time.

Now place the four pieces of aluminum-covered cardboard around the cup. Use books or rocks to prop the cardboard at an angle. Adjust the angle so that the foil catches the sunlight and reflects it onto the water.

Wait another 15 minutes and measure the water temperature. Write the time and temperature in your notebook.

What happens to the temperature of the water? Is it warmer each time you measure it? Why?

When a cup of water sits by itself in the Sun, it absorbs the heat from the Sun's rays and grows warmer. When you put the cardboard around the cup, the shiny aluminum reflects the Sun's rays toward the water, so it gets even warmer. The water absorbs more of the Sun's heat. If you want to investigate this effect in more detail, try these activities.

Try This: ✳ ✳ ✳ ✳ ✳ ✳ ✳ ✳ ✳ ✳

Measure the temperature of the air and write it down. Then fill a glass with cool water and measure the water temperature. Using a watch, see how long it takes the water to warm up to air temperature. What is the warmest the water gets without putting the aluminum-covered cardboard around it?

Try This: ✳ ✳ ✳ ✳ ✳ ✳ ✳ ✳ ✳ ✳

Put the aluminum-covered cardboard around the cup of water from the previous activity and continue to measure the temperature. How high does the temperature rise? How long does it take to reach its highest point?

Shadows

The Sun is brighter than anything else in the sky. It is, of course, the Sun's brightness that causes daylight. But the Sun also plays a part in some of the darkness we see around us. The Sun helps make shadows. Think about when you most often see shadows outside. Do you usually see them on very sunny days? When it's cloudy, there isn't enough sunlight to create a good shadow.

What is a shadow? A shadow is an area that is dark because something is blocking light from it. You might find shadows next to a tree or a building. The sunlight cannot get to the shadow area because the tree or building is in the way. Shadows can also be created by blocking other kinds of light, such as lamps, fires, or flashlights. Let's look at shadows created by the Sun.

Shadows fall according to the Sun's position in the sky.

Go out early in the morning before 9 o'clock on a sunny day. Do you see many shadows? Find an open spot with plenty of sunlight. Make sure there are no trees or buildings nearby that could block the Sun later in the day. There should be a sidewalk or other section of concrete that you have permission to mark with chalk.

With a piece of chalk, mark off a small circle about 2 inches (5 cm) in diameter. This will be the center of your *experiment.*

Get a yardstick or a meterstick. If you don't have one, you can use any long stick instead. Put one end of your stick on the circle and hold the other end up straight. Is your stick casting a shadow?

With your chalk, mark a line along the shadow on the concrete. If you can't hold the stick and mark the shadow at the same time, use a shorter stick, or ask a friend to hold the stick for you. Or you can simply mark where the shadow ends. Then you can put the stick down and draw a straight line from the mark to the circle.

Measure the length of the line you just drew. This is the length of the shadow. Write it down along with the time of day.

You will make more measurements later in the day. If you are doing your experiment in a playground or other public place, it might be a good idea to write a note in chalk asking people not to disturb your experiment.

At noon, go back to the same spot and measure the stick's shadow again. Measure it again later in the afternoon after 3 o'clock.

What happens to the shadow in the course of the day? Does your shadow get shorter and then longer again? Is it always in the same place, or does it move? Why do you think this happens?

The shadow changes because the position of the

Sun in the sky changes throughout the day. Early in the morning, the Sun appears low in the eastern sky. At this point, the length of your stick faces the Sun. So it blocks a lot of the light. That means the shadow is long. Shadows fall in the direction opposite the light source, so your shadow should be pointing mostly toward the west.

At noon, the Sun appears higher in the sky. In fact, at noon the Sun is close to its highest point in the sky for the day. At this time, the tip of your stick faces the Sun. So it blocks only a little bit of the light. Your shadow should be much smaller at noon than in the morning.

This shadow should not point much to either the east or the west since the Sun is in the middle of its path across the sky. It does point to the north, however, if you live in North America. That's because the Sun appears in the southern half of the sky. (If you live far south of the *equator*, your shadow will point south.)

With your chalk, draw an arrow that points in the direction opposite your shadow. This arrow points south if you live in

North America. It will come in handy when you do the activities on sundials and stars.

Late in the afternoon, the Sun again appears low in the sky. The length of the stick again blocks off the light. So the shadow should be long. But now the Sun is in the western sky. Your shadow should be pointing mostly toward the east.

Try This: ✳ ✳ ✳ ✳ ✳ ✳ ✳ ✳ ✳ ✳

Do the same experiment, but instead of a stick, use your own body. Get a friend to help you trace your body's shadow at different times of the day. Use chalk of a different color for each tracing.

Do the experiment in a darkened room with a flashlight or lamp. Can you move your light source in the same way the Sun appears to move across the sky?

Making a Sundial

By noticing where the Sun appears in the sky, people have always been able to get an idea of what time it is. But it's hard to get an exact time from looking at the Sun. And as we have said before, it's never a good idea to look directly at the Sun, even for just a second. So clocks are a very useful invention.

The slanting bar's shadow marks the time of day on this sundial.

But you can build an old-fashioned clock that works with the Sun. This *sundial* will give you a pretty accurate reading of the time.

Try This: ✳ ✳ ✳ ✳ ✳ ✳ ✳ ✳ ✳ ✳

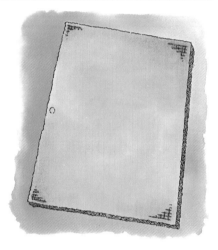

Get a piece of cardboard about 8 inches by 10 inches (20 cm by 25 cm). Halfway down one of the long edges of the cardboard, draw a small circle close to the edge on one side of the cardboard. Put a small ball of modeling clay on the circle.

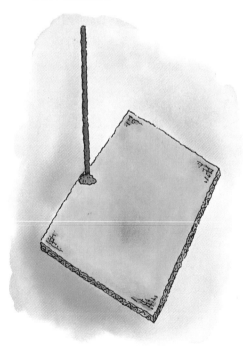

Get a short stick and push one end of it into the clay. Mold the clay around the stick to keep it standing upright. The stick should be as close to vertical as possible.

At 9 A.M. on a clear day, go outside and find a sunny spot. If you did the first activity on shadows, do this one in the same spot. Place your cardboard on the ground, with the stick standing upright. Rotate the cardboard so that the edge with the stick faces south. To find south, use the arrow you drew in the first shadow activity.

The stick should cast a shadow across your cardboard and onto the ground beyond. With a pen, mark the point where the shadow goes off the cardboard. It should be along one of the three edges without the stick.

With a ruler, draw a straight line from the circle to the mark you just made. Now label this line "9 A.M."

At 10 A.M., mark the shadow position again. Label the line "10 A.M." Do this every hour until late in the afternoon.

When you are finished, your cardboard should have a line for every hour you measured. The line for 12 noon should be in about the middle of the cardboard. However, that may depend on what time of year it is. In many places, people set their clocks ahead one hour in the spring so that it is light later in the evening throughout the summer. This practice is called Daylight Saving Time. If you are on Daylight Saving Time, the noon line would be shifted over about an hour from the middle of the cardboard.

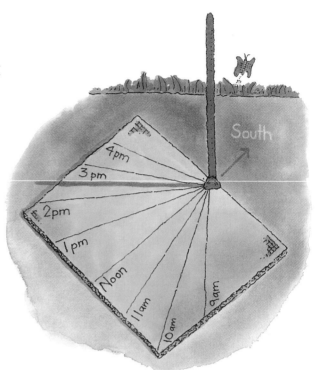

You now have a sundial. On the next sunny day, take your sundial outside at any time of the day. Again, place the cardboard on the ground with the stick side facing south. See where the stick's shadow falls. Is the shadow on one of the lines you drew?

If it is, read its label to see what time it is. If the shadow is between two lines, try estimating the time. For example, if it falls about halfway between 2 and 3 P.M., you might guess that it's 2:30. Check with a watch to see how accurate your sundial is.

Your sundial can be a handy and inexpensive clock to have around. But it won't always be useful. When won't your sundial be able to tell you the time?

SUNRISE AND SUNSET

In the previous activities, you saw that the Sun constantly changes position in the sky. Although it looks as if the Sun is moving across the sky, it is actually the Earth that is moving. The Earth *rotates*, or spins around,

This photograph shows the position of the Sun every five minutes as it sets over an observatory in the Canary Islands.

once every 24 hours. We move with the Earth as it rotates while the Sun stays in place.

It's a lot like riding on a carousel. As people standing on the ground go by, it may seem that they are the ones who are moving, not you. Similarly, it seems that the Sun is moving, not the Earth.

We can see the Sun during only part of the rotation. As the Earth continues to rotate, the Sun disappears from the sky in the west. This is what we call *sunset*. But the Sun has not actually "gone down." Our part of the Earth has just turned away from the Sun. When it is night where we live, the Sun shines on the opposite side of the Earth. The Earth rotates for another 9 to 15 hours before our part of the Earth once again turns toward the Sun. Then it is morning, or *sunrise*.

Sunrise and sunset occur at different times in different parts of the world. The timing of sunrise and sunset also changes with the seasons throughout the year. What time did you get up this morning? Was the Sun already up when you awoke? Or was it still dark outside? Will it still be light out at dinnertime today? Or will the Sun have already set by the time you're eating?

You can answer these questions by keeping track of the times of sunrise and sunset. How can you do this? You could watch the sky early every morning and at the end of every day. But that might interfere with school, your sleep, or dinner. Here is an easier way.

Try This: ✶ ✶ ✶ ✶ ✶ ✶ ✶ ✶ ✶

Just about *every* daily newspaper lists the time of sunrise and the time of sunset for the surrounding area. It's usually listed with the weather. See if you can find it in your parents' newspaper. Television weather reporters often give these times, too.

Then make a sunrise and sunset chart. At the top of a piece of paper, write the following:

Date   Time of Sunrise   Time of Sunset   Hours of Daylight

At sunrise, the Sun appears to move above the horizon.
But this is caused by the Earth's movement, not the Sun's.

✳ ✳ ✳ ✳ ✳ ✳ ✳ ✳ ✳ ✳ ✳ ✳ ✳ ✳

Write the day's date and the times of sunrise and sunset in the correct columns. Figure out the hours and minutes of daylight by subtracting the time of sunrise from the time of sunset. The easiest way to do this is to figure the hours and minutes separately.

For example, if sunrise is at 6:08 A.M. and sunset is at 7:42 P.M., count the number of hours from 6:08 A.M. to 7:08 P.M. (We stop at 7:08 P.M. because it is the closest hour to sunset without going past it.) You should count 7:08, 8:08, 9:08, 10:08, 11:08, 12:08, 1:08, 2:08, 3:08, 4:08, 5:08, 6:08, 7:08. Your answer would be 13 hours. Then subtract 8 minutes from 42 to get 34 minutes. The Daylight column should read 13 hours 34 minutes.

It's a little trickier when the minutes in the sunrise time are greater than the minutes in the sunset time. If the sunrise is at 6:31 A.M. and sunset at 7:12 P.M., for example, you would count 12 hours of daylight until 6:31 P.M. But to get the minutes, you'd have to subtract 31 from 12. This is a lot easier if you think of 7:00 P.M. as 6:60 P.M. That would mean 7:12 is 6:72. So you would subtract 31 from 72. Your answer would be 12 hours and 41 minutes.

Your chart might start out like this:

Date	Time of Sunrise	Time of Sunset	Hours of Daylight
April 20	6:09	7:41	13 hrs. 32 min.
April 21	6:08	7:42	13 hrs. 34 min.

Keep track of the sunrise and sunset every day for a few weeks, or longer if you'd like. You should begin to see some important patterns of change. As your chart grows, ask yourself these questions:

Is sunrise getting earlier or later?

Is sunset getting earlier or later?

Are the hours of daylight growing longer or shorter?

How many daylight hours are there on the first day of a new season?

Does the amount of daylight change when you set your clocks forward in the spring or back in the fall?

You can answer these questions even if you keep track of the sunrise and sunset only *every few days* or once a week. Why do these patterns happen? The answer has to do with the tilt of the Earth and its movement around the Sun. While the Earth is rotating, it is also *revolving*, or traveling in a big circle, around the Sun. It takes only a day for the Earth to make one rotation, but 365 days (a year) to make one revolution of the Sun!

In part of the Earth's travel around the Sun, the North Pole is tilted slightly away from the Sun. In North America, the Sun appears low in the southern sky at this time. This means North America gets little daylight and long, cold nights. In other words, it causes our winter. When it is summer in North America, the North Pole is tilted slightly toward the sun. This means the Sun appears in a long, high path across the sky. So we get long, hot days and shorter nights. If you live in South America it works the opposite way.

THE MOON

The Sun is always the brightest object in the daytime sky. But at night the brightest object might be a planet or a star, which is a faraway sun. Or it might be the moon. The moon looks a lot larger than the stars in the

At night, the moon rises and sets like the Sun does. Here, a half-moon is setting.

sky. Why, then, isn't it always the brightest object? Because sometimes we can't see the moon in the sky at night. The Sun is in the sky every day, although the clouds sometimes block it. So why isn't the moon always in the night sky? And why is it always changing shape?

To find out more about the moon, let's do some moon-watching. Luckily, we can look at the moon all we like. It cannot hurt our eyes because its light is not as strong as the Sun's. However, the moon's light actually comes from the Sun. At night, the Sun is on the other side of the Earth. But its light shines on the moon and bounces down to us on Earth.

Try This: ✳ ✳ ✳ ✳ ✳ ✳ ✳ ✳ ✳ ✳

Find a good place to watch the sky at night. It might be a window in your house or apartment. Or it might be a place outside that gives you a clear view of the sky. This activity may be easier to do in the summer when it's warm outside at night and when you can stay up later.

From this spot, check for the moon every night. It may take a while until you see it because, as we said, it's not always visible at night. And sometimes it's not visible until after you are asleep.

Once you have seen the moon, draw a picture of it on paper, in your notebook, or on a calendar. Below your picture, write the date and the time you saw the moon.

The next night, look for the moon at the same time of night. If you can see it, it's probably not in the same place in the sky as the night before. If the sky is clear

and you can't see the moon at all, wait about an hour. It should show up. When it does, draw its picture and write down the date and time.

Keep watching the sky and drawing your pictures of the moon. You may have to look later and later each night. If it gets past your bedtime, you can actually look for the moon in the daytime sky in the morning. The moon is often out at daytime. It's just harder to see it in the bright light of the Sun.

Why isn't the moon always in the same place in the sky at the same time every night? The moon travels in a circle around the Earth every 28 days. So after the Earth has made one rotation in a day, the moon has traveled a little bit further in its path around our planet. The Earth has to rotate for almost another hour before the moon appears in the same place in the sky as it did the night before.

Because the moon revolves around the Earth, the moon rises and sets at different times just like the Sun does. In the previous activity, we saw that the times of sunrise and sunset change only a minute or two each day. But the times of moonrise and moonset change almost an hour every day.

Did the moon change shape from night to night while you were watching it? Why does that happen?

Earlier we said that the moon's light is actually light from the Sun reflecting off the moon. But sometimes we can't see all the light reflecting off the moon. It all depends on where the moon is in its orbit, or path, around the Earth.

If the moon is on the side of the Earth away from the Sun, we can see the whole side of the moon that is lit by the Sun. That is what we call a full moon. If the moon is in a spot where we can see only half of the lit side, we call it a half-moon. If we see even less than that, it's a crescent moon. Sometimes only the dark side of the moon faces the Earth and we see nothing at all. We call that a new moon.

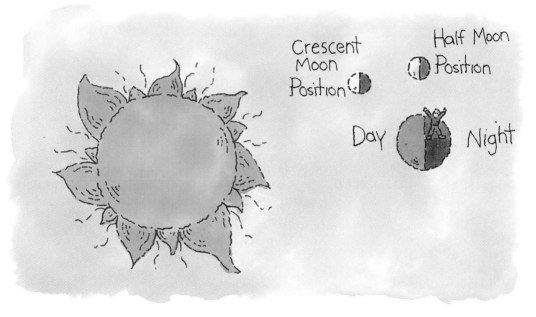

After the full moon appears, we see a little bit less of the reflected sunlight each night until we can't see any of the moon at all. When the moon has made a complete orbit, we start to see a little more of it each night, and the cycle begins all over again.

THE STARS

For thousands of years people have looked up at the night sky and stared in wonder at the beauty of the heavens. Stars have always fascinated people. Some people have spent a great deal of time trying to figure out what the stars are, how far away they are, and how they got there.

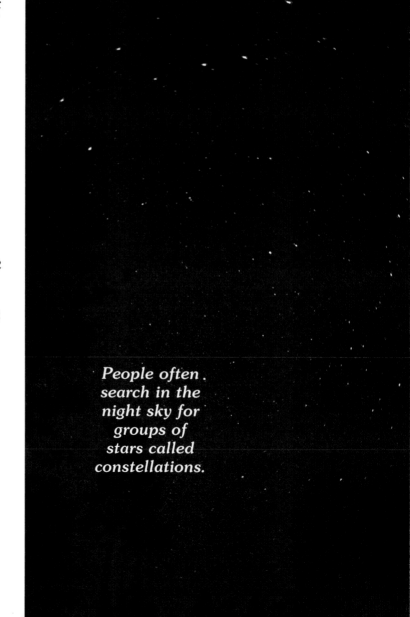

People often search in the night sky for groups of stars called constellations.

The Greeks and other people in ancient times saw groups of stars that looked like animals or characters from their stories. To help organize their knowledge of the stars, they named each group of stars after an animal or character. These groups of stars are called *constellations*.

Even after a couple of thousand years, astronomers still use many of the ancient names. Would you like to find some of these constellations?

Try This: ✳ ✳ ✳ ✳ ✳ ✳ ✳ ✳ ✳ ✳

Go outside on a clear, moonless night. Find an open spot where you can see as much of the sky as possible. Look to the northern sky. (If you don't know where north is, look in the direction opposite the arrow you

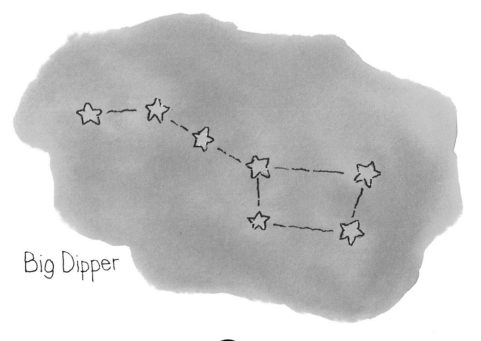

Big Dipper

drew in the activity on page 17. Use a compass or ask an adult if you didn't do the activity.)

Look first for the Big Dipper. The Big Dipper looks like a cooking pot with a bent handle. You may have to look for a while to find it. It is not always in the same place in the northern sky. The Big Dipper is part of a larger constellation called Ursa Major, or Great Bear.

Once you have found the Big Dipper, you can easily find the Little Dipper. Just move your eyes along the line of the two stars at the front of the pot. Take your eyes above the pot and you will come to the tip of the handle of the Little Dipper. The Little Dipper is part of a larger constellation called Ursa Minor, or Little Bear. Now look carefully in

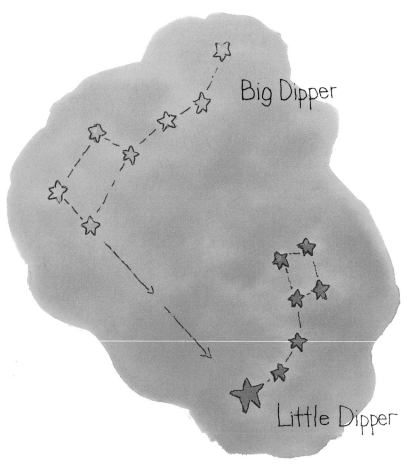

Big Dipper

Little Dipper

the space between the Big Dipper and the Little Dipper. You should find a string of stars that leads to four stars in the shape of a diamond. This constellation is called

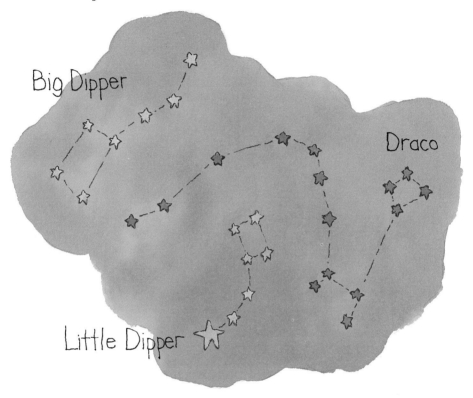

Draco, or the dragon. The diamond is the head of the dragon and the string of stars is its body.

If you follow the dragon's neck down in a line across the sky, you will come to a zigzagging constellation in the shape of the letter W. It is called *Cassiopeia*, the name of an Ethiopian queen in ancient times. It was probably named Cassiopeia because the stars are quite bright, like a queen's crown.

If you have a clear view of the sky, you should be

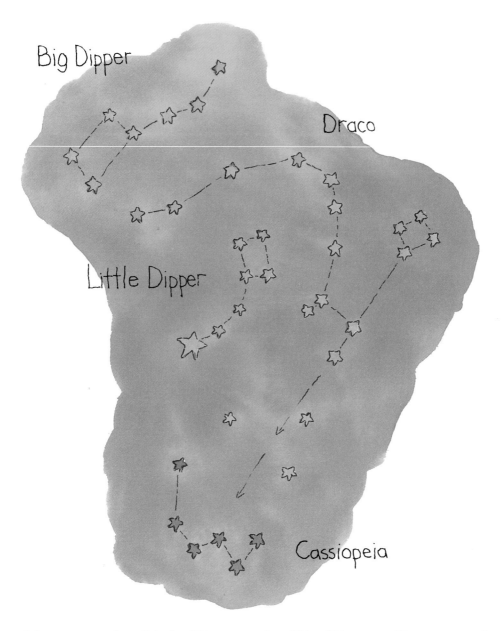

Big Dipper

Draco

Little Dipper

Cassiopeia

able to see the Little Dipper, the Big Dipper, Draco, and Cassiopeia all year round. They are in different parts of the sky throughout the year, but you can always find them next to each other.

Can you find the Big Dipper?

The stars change location in the sky for the same reason the Sun appears to move across the sky. The Earth rotates once each day and also moves in a circle around the Sun over the course of a year. It may seem that the stars move, but we are the ones who are moving. To us, the stars appear to move across the sky together.

All the constellations in this activity were found by the Greeks. Other groups of people have seen their own pictures in the stars. You can invent your own constellations, too.

Take a notebook or paper outside on a clear night and stare up at the sky. Let your imagination run loose. See what pictures your mind can create from the stars. Look for groups of stars that remind you of a person, an animal—or anything at all. Do you see a creature, a hero, a city?

Draw the stars as they appear in your constellation. Then name your constellation. Think about a story that could go along with your picture. Write the story down when you get back inside. Keep the story with your picture.

See if you can find your constellation on different nights throughout the year.

The North Star

For hundreds of years sailors traveled across the seas without instruments to tell them which direction they were going. One of their most important guides across the northern seas was a single star. It is called Polaris, or the North Star. The North Star is well named, for it always appears in the northern sky. That is why it is such a reliable guide.

As we said before, most other stars appear in different parts of the sky over the course of a year. But since the North Star is in the sky above the North Pole, it always appears in the north. The Earth rotates around a line, or an axis, running from the North Pole to the South Pole. While the land close to the equator moves a lot, the poles do not move. So no matter how much the Earth has rotated, the North Star stays above the North Pole.

Sailors and other travelers could find the North Star in the sky and be sure that the direction it pointed was north. Today ships have radars, computers, and satellites to guide them.

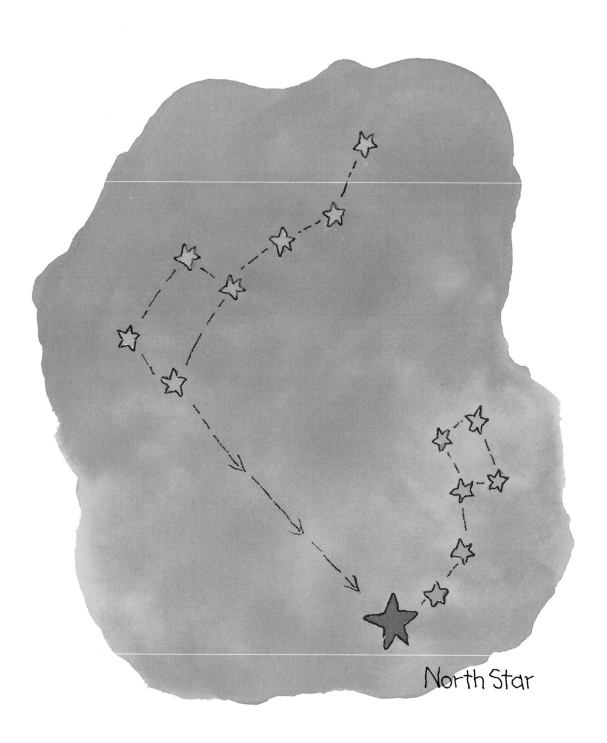

North Star

To find the North Star, wait until it's dark enough to see lots of stars. The North Star is the very last star on the Little Dipper's handle.

The easiest way to find the North Star is to find the Big Dipper first in the northern sky. As in the previous activity, follow the two stars at the front of the dipper up and away from the pot. They will point you right towards the North Star. It is brighter than the other stars in the Little Dipper's handle.

Now that you know exactly where north is, can you figure out where the other three compass directions are?

Try doing this in different locations and at different times of the year.

BECOMING AN ASTRONOMER

The wonders of the day and night skies are endless. If you keep watching the sky, you are sure to find out more about the stars and planets that will amaze you. When you see something unusual in the sky, write it down in your notebook. Write down anything you notice about it and any questions you have about it. Then investigate to find out why it happens.

You may have to do some research at the library to find the answer. Or you may be able to get the answer from a teacher or parent. Record the answers in your notebook.

This is what real astronomers do. If you find that you enjoy these activities, start reading news stories about what other astronomers are doing. New discoveries and explorations are made every year. You may be able to go to an observatory and see some of them through a telescope. You can get a better look at the planets that way, too.

If you watch the sky through a telescope, you may see a comet like this one.

But the most important thing to do is keep your eyes open and watch the sky!

GLOSSARY

astronomer (uh-STRAH-nuh-mer)—a person who studies stars, planets, and other objects in space.

Cassiopeia (kas-see-uh-PEE-uh)—a constellation named after an Ethiopian queen.

constellation (KON-stuh-LAY-shun)—a group of stars that have been given a name because of their arrangement or pattern.

diameter (DIE-AM-uh-ter)—the distance across a circle as measured through its center. It indicates the size of the circle.

Draco (DRAY-koh)—a constellation that is shaped like a dragon.

equator (ee-KWAY-ter)—a geographical line circling the Earth, dividing it into northern and southern halves. The Sun appears to move back and forth across the equator during the year.

experiment (ik-SPEAR-uh-ment)—a test that a scientist carries out to discover information about something.

orbit (OR-bit)—the circular path of a moon or planet around another astronomical body.

revolve (rih-VOLV)—to move in a circle around another object.

rotate (ROW-tate)—to spin in a circle.

sundial (SUN-dial)—an old-fashioned clock that uses a shadow cast by the Sun to tell time.

sunrise—the time at the beginning of the day when the Sun peeks over the horizon.

sunset—the time at the end of the day just before the Sun sinks entirely below the horizon.

telescope (TEL-uh-skope)—an instrument that magnifies objects such as planets so that astronomers can see them.

temperature (TEM-per-uh-chure)—the measure of how warm or cold an object is.

thermometer (ther-MAH-muh-ter)—an instrument for measuring temperature.

INDEX

Page numbers in *italics* indicate illustrations.